The Trilogy

- BOOK TWO -

I0088355

Mystery Civilizations

Seth Returns Publishing
Lake County California

Published by Seth Returns Publishing
Lake County California

Editorial: Mark Allen Frost
Cover Art, Design, Typography & Layout: Mark Frost

Library of Congress Control Number: 2010904958

ISBN: 978-0-9826946-0-2

This book is dedicated with love and gratitude to The Warrior. Thanks for everything Dad.

Many thanks to Walter Zweifel, Klaus Shulte and Boris N. Krivoruk for their generous contributions to this project.

CONTENTS

Introduction by Mark............................*ix*
Introduction by Seth............................*xi*
Remembering the Ancient Wisdom......*xiii*
Preface...*xv*

CHAPTER ONE

ANIZASI...1

CHAPTER TWO

ANNUNAKI...7

CHAPTER THREE

ATLANTIS...11

CHAPTER FOUR

GA..29

CHAPTER FIVE

HUNZA..49

CHAPTER SIX

LEMURIA..55

CHAPTER SEVEN

MAYAN...61

CHAPTER EIGHT

MU..67

CHAPTER NINE

NIAMENNON...71

CHAPTER TEN

SETI...75

CHAPTER ELEVEN

SUMARI..83

CHAPTER TWELVE

BEST CASE SCENARIO..89

CONTENTS

Epilogue...*91*

Ritual of Sanctuary...........................*93*

Glossary...*95*

Ordering Page...................................*100*

INTRODUCTION BY MARK

Welcome to the new Seth book. This one is the result of conversations we had with visitors to our website. A couple of years ago Seth suggested we ask visitors to sethreturns.com to submit questions on what he calls the Mystery Civilizations. Readers from New Zealand, Canada, Australia, the U.S. and Asia responded with questions. Because Seth had commented on Atlantis, GA, and Lemuria in his last two books, I asked him to follow up on those comments.

The material that Seth has given us here is fantastic and intriguing. Most of it is new information, not to be found in any book anywhere. In this book in particular, Seth is definitely challenging our basic theories of what reality is and how it is created.

I would like to pass along a couple of recent quotes from Seth from when I asked him about this material. I was expressing doubt and asking for encouragement and verification.

MYSTERY CIVILIZATIONS

These collectives represent future development as well as past. Your focus on them in your present Moment Point, facilitates the remembering process.

And this one...

Citizens of the Mystery Civilizations experience bleedthroughs to your modern culture and are amazed at what they see. They are seeing the modern world through your eyes. When you experience a bleedthrough into their existence, you are seeing their civilization through their eyes. It is a synchrony of perception, you see, that facilitates these dimensional-breakthroughs between you and your Simultaneous Lives

I know what Seth is getting at here, and I hope Seth's readers can see it too. He expects a lot of his readers in this new material. Good Luck with it.

.

INTRODUCTION BY SETH

Seth would you like to work on Mystery Civilizations?

Yes Mark. It has been some time. However, as you know, the information is always there for you to "download" into your consciousness. A moment…

The past, as you conceive of it, Dear Reader, seems to be quite stable. It seems to be a completed act, or series of acts, that exists beyond any sort of interventions of change you might wish to carry out from your current timeframe. "The past cannot be changed," remains a dictum for you in 3D Reality.

Yet the permanence of the past is simply an assumption on your part. It is a root assumption that allows you to assist in the ongoing fabrication of your camouflage reality. It is a mis-perception that we hope to correct for you within your own Personal Reality Field.

Now, I am flinging about various words and phrases here that will have meaning for you only if you have read some of my books. Therefore, if you do not understand what I am talking about in these pages, go back to the early material, the foundational material from your past. If you do this, it will allow me the freedom in these new works to simply stand upon my soapbox, you see, and begin the oration. (humorously)

Yet let me assure you, that this book will not be all inclusive with regards to the Mystery Civilizations. There are numerous of these civilizations that have existed, and indeed, are existing on your Earth. You may remember from our earlier discussions with you, that it is our assertion that it is consciousness that creates reality. Each thought seeks out manifestation of itself. Your <u>collective</u> thoughts give birth to civilizations upon your Earth and elsewhere.

Now you are you the reader currently in this moment of awareness. You ARE reading this book. You ARE a citizen of Earth in your modern timeframe. We wrote this book for YOU. Yet we are hoping that you may also realize this simple yet profound idea: you are ALSO, within the same precise assemblage of Consciousness Units that comprise your physical body, experiencing OTHER lives. Some of these lives are being lived within the Mystery Civilizations that we will describe to you shortly. This is an intimate journey of discovery for you, then. We hope to gently lead you forward in this endeavor.

REMEMBERING THE ANCIENT WISDOM

There is much talk in your media about getting in touch with past lives. Dear Reader, you are already in touch with your past lives. They inform each and every moment of your current existence. These past lives include lives lived within what we are calling the Mystery Civilizations, as well as other of your Simultaneous Existences that are ongoing throughout your past, your present, and your future.

Not only are we asking you to accept this data as true within your Personal Reality, we are also suggesting to you that you may, with just minimal effort on your part, explore YOUR contribution to some or all of the Mystery Civilizations. For it is our contention that you have spent several lifetimes within these unknown worlds. It was there that you learned firsthand the secrets of the universe. You learned, for example, that you do indeed create your own reality: that you have the creative energies of the Logos at your disposal, in other words.

Through these other lives, you are again-and-again re-acquainted with your own power, in that you are always born with the amnesia that prevents you from remembering your other lives. Then, as you live the life of a seeker of knowledge, let us say, you "remember" these Lessons learned in your Simultaneous Existences. You may be in a familiar place here and now as you read these words. You may be remembering this Ancient Wisdom once again in this timeframe. If this is so for you, I suggest you take it with a grain of salt, as you say. From my perspective, this is merely another opportunity for you to seek out the mysteries of your existence and share your findings with others: humbly, you see, with Courage and Loving Understanding.

PREFACE

We are assuming here, that the reader already has some sense of how to explore their Inner World. As a Scientist of Consciousness, you would already be somewhat skilled at entering the Trance State at will. You would also be working on your Issues in physical reality, the Lessons that humans incarnate to learn. This manuscript is experiential, then. It is a workbook, as are the majority of my new books I am writing. It is expected that the reader wishes to be engaged in the exploration of these other worlds, perhaps because they have a feeling they have lived within one of these societies, and wishes to confirm this for themselves.

To this end, all of our books in this series will be small volumes compared to our first works on the awakening of humanity. These short volumes are being created with most of the theory and ephemera missing. We are providing for you the reader, a concise compendium of information on these Lost Civilizations. We are hoping that you will be inspired to take this little book with you as you go about your daily excursions in physical reality, using it as a reference in the field, as you conduct your experiments within your life.

CHAPTER ONE

The Anizasi

I would be very interested in anything concerning the Anizasi of the American South West and the origins of North American tribes. ~ Jacquie Shockley

Inter-dimensional Beings

This is an excellent question. Let me answer this question in a general way without naming names, as in specific tribes, for the list of civilizations that preceded the North American tribes would fill this volume.

I am speaking of the probable manifestations of large human groups, here. This is how your consensus realities are crafted: through the selection of Reality Constructs from the limitless field of probable constructs by the people of a given area. The reality constructs are given life by individuals. The civilization is enlivened by large groups of individuals.

Now let us talk about origins. The North American tribes are and were the descendants of inter-dimensional beings from beyond the solar system that includes Earth. The way this occurs is this: as in all manifestations of the individual human form upon Earth, the Soul Self of particular Entities of consciousness associated with All That Is, send out a seed to grow within the baby, the human baby. It is not productive to ask which came first, the human baby or the transmission of the spark of All That Is into the consciousness of the baby. Everything exists at once. Linear time is an illusion. However, let me give you some background information on this process of birthing a civilization.

The Star People

The myths of the North American tribes are quite often literal descriptions of what took place in their inception. The Star People figure quite large in these descriptions of tribal origins. These narratives describe events that occurred on the inner world of the unconscious - the Underworld. Thus you have the predominance of essential symbols of great power. Now the birth of civilizations entails a mass inception of a great many sparks of Soul into the bodies of human beings - babies and otherwise.

The question of what existed before this mass inception can be answered quite simply: previous civilizations existed before this mass inception. In the same way, a multitude of after-occurring civilizations existed simultaneously before this mass inception. To illustrate: the current residents of North America, including the Native Peoples, the Americans, the Canadians and the Latin Americans, are the current manifestation of these Mystery Civilizations. All of these civilizations exist simultaneously, outside of time as you perceive it.

I sense Jacquie that you require some details of confirmation and validation. I will attempt to provide these elements for you. In all of the cultures of your world, there are noted within their ancient histories, the activities of the magic ancestors. To the modern scientist including the anthropologist and others, these stories are conceived as myths: symbolic narratives having no REAL basis in physical reality. In my new books I have made the statement that everything conceived by consciousness has a very real reality, including these so-called myths. Consciousness, in the form of ideas, images, emotion-powered concepts, creates itself in physical form or in dimensions other than the physical.

Magic Ancestors

The Anizasi are noted for their wonderworking. They are the magic ancestors. In this case, the activities of these proto-scientists have been documented and are now part of the "historical" record. Yet I am not exaggerating when I tell you that EVERY group, every civilization from your perceived past, exists simultaneously with its magic ancestors manifesting at the same time. The magic ancestors exist in an adjacent dimension. This dimension is connected to the Third Dimension through portals of communication some of you call chakras. These doorways into other dimensions may be accessed by the interested explorer of non-physical reality through techniques perfected by magicians, shamans, witches and healers over the ages.

There is a reason you are interested in the Anizasi people. You are connected to these people and you are attempting to "find your way back home." Home for you then would be a star system that is as yet unidentified by your scientists. This planetary system is quite similar to the solar system in which your Earth resides. An assortment of planetary bodies revolves around a nurturing star. Life of many forms exists upon these planets. I have referred to these other systems as simply "dimensions" to assist the reader in finding the necessary wherewithal to "visit" these domains in their meditations. I have defined extraterrestrial as extra-dimensional, for this is a truer assessment. You will not need a spaceship to visit these other systems, only your creative consciousness.

Envoy of the Sacred

Your star system is hidden from view by other systems. I commented on this in my book on ***Soul Evolu-***

tion. Your North American tribes originated from this star system. Inter-dimensional travel is instantaneous, in that one moment, the subject is existing on their home planet and in the next, they are living their life upon Earth, many light years from home, in your terms. To extend this description somewhat: the subject here would not be surprised or traumatized by this event. The subject, as an Etheric Being, would know quite well what was in store for them. They would know that they were to travel to Earth as an envoy of the sacred, All That Is, to assist in the creation of a civilization.

Some of these beings traveled to the Third Dimension of Earth to serve as members of the Spiritual Hierarchy. This group serves humanity as the intermediaries between the physical and non-physical worlds. They are the beings that have been personalized by humanity to act as various gods, goddesses, and other sacred beings.

These sacred beings, then, served as the Gestalts of Consciousness – the energy blueprints – for the creation of the spiritual world of the Native American tribes and indeed for many of the tribes of the South American continent. This simply means that the origin myths of the aboriginal tribes are not "imagined" - they are not the product of the ingestion of herbs and other potent sacraments, though these have certainly assisted the psychic voyagers within these tribes in identifying and cataloguing the divine spirits – they are as real as any other perceived/created Reality Construct you would care to name.

Further Explorations

Now we shall go much further in these descriptions of the magic ancestors and the mythologies of your Mystery Civilizations in later writings. Here I will complete my description with a summary: Your Anizasi are the magic ancestors of the North and South American tribes. This collective of spirit beings exists within your collective consciousness and may be contacted through ritual and other forms of experimentation. I trust you have received the information you requested.

CHAPTER TWO

The Annunaki

Are we enslaved by the Annunaki? There is an author who says we were enslaved from the beginning. Is the Annunaki at it again? ~ Cynthia Hill

Negative Entities

Certainly these beings exist within their own dimension of experiencing Mark. These are the Negative Entities we speak of in our work. This particular expression within physical reality, the Annunaki, was thought of as extraterrestrial in origin – "from another planet," as you say - and indeed this was their genesis originally. Yet you well know that ALL OF YOU, all of the Earth beings, have come from other systems originally.

Your Earth is quite young compared to the other planets and other environments that hold upon them the living organisms. These Negative Entities, the Annunaki, are quite ancient.

Now this collective was not completely embodied within physical reality as you think of it. Their consciousness did not seek out complete expression within human form. The main expression was one of concerted influence upon the mental functioning of the residents of Earth in order to control "productivity."

Over the generations, then, we have the influence of this Negative Entity exerting control over humanity through the Negative Emotions. The Negative Entities, remember, thrive on the emotional states of fear, anger, anxiety, greed, ruthlessness. These negative Idea Constructs - composed of Consciousness Units, again I remind you – coalesce on the subtle levels where they act as blueprints for the fabrication of negative Realty Constructs.

The Negative Gods

The Annunaki may be thought of as the Gestalt of Consciousness that had the most influence on the Earth races with regards to the emotion of greed. This group is certainly not, strictly speaking, a Mystery Civilization, however the influence of these negative beings has been quite pronounced on all of Earth's civilizations. They are the inspiration for the negative gods within the religions of humanity, for example. There have been gods and goddesses representing the human virtues. These are in large part inspired by Beings of Light, Angels, and what have you. The gods and goddesses of darkness, of revenge, of hate and fear are always created from the idea constructs, images, and emotional content generated by the Annunaki energy gestalt.

Continuum of Consciousness

As I said, this is not technically a Mystery Civilization we are describing. Yet this does demonstrate the reality of evolutionary consciousness – of All That Is. We are reminded that the path of development much more resembles a continuum than a staged series of phenomena with discrete nameable societies existing within separate timeframes.

The Negative Entities have informed humanity forever, in your terms. They exist currently, in this moment, as probable evolutionary paths for the Soul Self. You are a physical being, yet you also inhabit the non-physical world. You are in constant contact with Entities of all types. These Annunaki influences, then, are quite pronounced in your collective consciousness currently. The manifestation of collective negative realities REQUIRES the direction and energetic support of this Gestalt of Consciousness. Through your free will choices, as you live your life in the modern world, you ally with different Entities. If you ally with the Negative Entities through entertaining negative thoughts, images, and emotions within your psyche, you endorse and strengthen the Negative Entities.

Specifically here: if you accept the information stream of greed, of ruthlessness, of murderous intent, into your mental sphere, you are effectively collaborating with the Negative Entities; you are assisting the Annunaki in their agenda of fear, anger, domination, and despair.

With regards to the claim that these Negative Entities are enslaving mankind, I must concur. I have stated before that the modern human is a slave to consumerism, to the buying of shiny objects. The activities of the Annunaki are feeding this desire to consume. Yet this group is merely another Gestalt of Consciousness that exists for you in your mental sphere. You could just as easily CHANGE YOUR PATTERN and choose to ally your Reality Creation energies with Beings of Light.

Slave to Consumerism

In other words: yes you are a slave to consumerism and the agenda of the Negative Entities, but YOU ARE ENSLAVING YOURSELF. The responsibility for your choices resides with you personally. It does not do to blame your society or some distant negative figure: "The devil made me do it." You are responsible. I will now discontinue my oration (humorously).

CHAPTER THREE

Atlantis

Regarding your explanation of Atlantis as being as much in our future as our past. Do you mean that it is largely a state of consciousness rather than a particular place and time, in linear terms? ~ Tim Bowden

A State of Consciousness

Yes Tim. We have discussed Atlantis in our Second book. Let me explain. A moment… From the perspective of your greater multidimensional being, Tim, EVERY-THING is ultimately a state of consciousness. All Reality Constructs that compose your individual and collective realities are composed of Consciousness Units that are essentially thoughts, ideas, beliefs, emotions etc. "solidified," in a sense, to create your world. So certainly, all of your created reality is a state of consciousness, a state of shared telepathic reality.

You cooperate with the CUs that compose not only your physical body but also do you cooperate with the CUs that compose the "stuff" that composes all that is

NOT you. Do you see? The Telepathic Network is the fertile ground upon which you plant your seeds of thought, to nurture them and indeed grow these seeds into their respective constructs.

Also let me say, that as a multidimensional being, one who lives many lives simultaneously, including some lives within the Mystery Civilizations, you are now in this moment contributing in very noticeable ways to the lives you are living everywhere. This is a delicate point I think. Let me go further.

Can you forget for just a moment here (humorously) your infatuation with linear time and your camouflage reality? If you are able to do this, you will see the truth. You are Tim in the current timeframe. Yes this is true. Yet you are also, for example, a human living a life within the Mystery Civilization you know as Atlantis. You may prove this to yourself by using your Inner Senses to tune-in to this other life. Let us say that you have done so and you are now getting glimpses – bleedthroughs – into this Simultaneous Life in Atlantis. You are experiencing the bleedthrough through the spacious moment – your current Moment Point.

Change the Past From the Current Moment

Now I would ask you Tim, what would be the "result" of your directing an intense stream of emotional energy -

of Love let us say – at this Atlantean life? Would you have an effect on the personality living this life? Let us assume for the moment that, yes you would have a subtle effect upon this life. Within the Gestalt of Consciousness that you participate in with all of your Reincarnational Existences, your thoughts may be intercepted by your Atlantean self. Then, also subtly perhaps, you might notice a change in behavior in this other life. Perhaps this other life is now musing upon the concept of Loving Understanding. Let us state here that, prior to the reception of this Loving thought complex, your Atlantean self was experiencing anger, perhaps hatred. Do you see how your etheric message from the future may assist a past existence in achieving a more positive state of consciousness?

Given this explanation, do you see how your current behaviors pave the way for altered realities within all of your Reincarnational Existences? Cumulatively, you might say that your current behaviors have such an influence on the "future," in your terms, manifestation of the Atlantean Civilization, that you could very well assist in redirecting the civilization from its catastrophic trajectory of development.

Now you change the past from the current moment. You do this naturally, subconsciously. You create BOTH past and future from within this spacious moment. Do you see how collectively, if the millions of you experiencing this current timeframe as well as the Atlantean existences, were to change your attitudes "all at once," that the mythological outcomes of Atlantis might become positive rather than negative historically. If this were to occur, you might see a wholesale alteration in the depiction of this "myth" in your books and other media. As a collective, you would be recreating a more positive manifestation of Atlantean Civilization, just as you perhaps may be influencing your current civilization in positive ways.

Seth can you tell us more about Atlantis? Just some highlights of the civilization and the conditions in which Atlantis was supposedly destroyed? ~ MF

Space and Time Are Fluid

Mark I have answered Tim's question rather generally and with a particular emphasis. Now I will answer your question with a different slant.

First Mark, the past is just as fluid as the future. Anything can happen in the past just as anything can happen in the future, in your terms. It is easier for you to accept that the future is more open to change than your past, for you are hypnotized by your consensus reality. However, if you would step out for just a moment, of your obsessively-created consensus reality, as I suggested to Tim, you would naturally begin to create independently.

Now to relate this to matters of Atlantis and its "fall." Your civilization Mark, the American Empire shall we say, exists, grows, survives simultaneously with the "preceding" empire occupied by your Native American tribes, as well as countless physical and probable manifestations of civilizations that occurred and are to occur on your world. All manifestations of these civilizations exist at once. The past, the present, and the future civilizations exist now, in this moment.

Let me add that questions of locales and sites of ancient civilizations need not have a bearing on these discussions. For not only is time simply a convenience for you in 3D Reality, but space is also. Again, you decide as a collective of human creators, where, when, and how you will create your individual lives, in what timeframes, and in what groupings or civilizations. You decide as a collective where your civilization of Atlantis will develop and has developed as well as the particulars of every aspect of that society.

Similarities in Lessons

We have spoken in our second book of the similarities in Lessons faced by the Atlanteans and by the modern developed nations. The use of Power with a capital P; the manifestation of Spirit, spirituality within the culture; the ethical use of technology.

Your modern civilization and your mystery civilization of Atlantis are engaged in the learning of similar Lessons, for both collectives of humans are of the same Entity of consciousness. In this way, you and the other members of your nation, as well as others in their developed nations on your Earth at this time, have the opportunity to indeed LEARN all these valuable Lessons, to the degree that the cataclysmic effects of your negative thoughts do not result in a global thermonuclear war - as I have warned you about in our new writings - or a tragic FALL of the Atlantean empire through earth changes - calamities brought on by these same negative thoughts within your "past" incarnations.

It all happens at once Mark. Each change of thought, emotion, and behavior toward the positive manifestation is reflected in ALL of your reincarnational existences, including those within the Mystery Civilizations. As you can see, I am again being rather vague. I am not allowed to interfere with the learning of your primary Lessons. You will either learn your Lessons individually and as a group or you will not. You decide.

Crystals

Now as a tidbit of intriguing data, I am allowed to comment further on some of the other aspects of Atlantean culture we hinted at in previous sessions. A moment…

The manufacture of "spun" crystalline material that had the properties of creating, storing and transmitting energy was perfected by Atlantean scientists. Common materials from the Earth were subjected to electro-magnetic forces to facilitate the crystallization of these minerals into implements of various sizes and intensities. The catalyst in this manufacturing process was an element as yet undiscovered by your modern researchers. It is an unknown element that exists extra-dimensionally. When the Fourth-Dimensional Shift is completed, your scientists using their Inner Senses, will discover this element within the common sand and soil of your planet.

These crystals were grown to lengths of one or two inches to great heights of 50 and one hundred feet. The large crystals were often ten or more feet in diameter. They were a dark ashen color, almost black, with the threads of the crystal composition visible within.

Time Travel

We covered Time Travel in *Thought Reality*. Now I shall add to that material in relation to the Atlantis civilization. The truth is, what you would call Time Travel was a common occurrence in the great civilizations of your perceived past. There are reasons for this, having to do with issues of shared spirituality, an appreciation for the natural forces of nature, and a cosmology shared by the people that allowed and even nurtured the exploring of non-physical reality. None of these features are shared by great numbers of you in your modern timeframe. That is why Time Travel, for the most part, is thought of as an impossibility: a joke.

The Atlantean researchers of non-physical reality perfected the spinning of crystalline structures into vehicles. The researcher would, as we said, place themselves within the structure and allow their Inner Senses to be amplified and tuned by the crystal mass. In this way, the Intention of the researcher to visit a particular timeframe was made manifest within their own mental environment. You may also compare this activity to the sacred voyages of shamans and other seekers of visions in your many world cultures. The effects are the same here. The technologies are different, that is all.

Death Ray

The crystals amplified and tuned human thought and emotion. For this reason, it was imperative that the operator be of the utmost integrity and emotional stability. I have stated that these crystals were used as communication and power transmitters. Imagine the consequences of allowing an unbalanced individual directing their emotional thought energy through a gigantic crystal transmitter. The results of these "mistakes" were documented in your mythologies as the wholesale destruction of populations through use of the "Death Ray." For the most part, these tragedies were unintentional.

Whales and Dolphins

Just pick up the thread, Mark... The connections to whales and dolphins that have been dramatized in your consensus reality manifestations of the Atlantis "mythology," were and are quite real connections. In your stories of Atlantis, particularly those told by your New Agers, the whales and dolphins are thought of as the present timeframe incarnations of the Atlantean people. In some way, the story goes, Atlantis was destroyed, but the people of Atlantis "live on" in the bodies of these sea creatures.

Let me explain for you how this particular relationship of man-to-animal first began and endures. In societies that predated Atlantis and most of the Mystery Civilizations we are covering in this manuscript, the divisions between human and animal consciousness were not as clearly defined as those separations devised by modern man. The human consciousness was a great deal more fluid than currently. Modern man, the scientists among you, would describe this relationship of man to animal as imaginal, created out of a need to hold some influence over the beasts of the Earth, so that they may better track these animals and take them for food. This symbiotic relationship between man and his prey did and does exist for you in your collective awareness. In your tribal cultures it is a given that the animals hunted to sustain life for the tribe are reciprocally aware of this "divine" relationship.

The ancients were quite aware of their innate divinity. They sensed their connection to their environment and to the animals and other inhabitants of their world. The living beings also include the stones, the trees, all of the "stuff" that constitutes the world of the Third-Dimensional human. Everything is alive, conscious, connected. I am sure you are quite well aware of this fact by now.

The Atlanteans were oriented outward into the surrounding seas and oceans. They were explorers and navigators of the world around them and developed fleets of sturdy vessels that they used to carry goods to trade with others in their area and even much farther away, as in many hundreds of miles out to sea. Perhaps you can see where I am taking this Mark. These seagoing explorers and traders of Atlantis, having a certain "instinct" you might say, for ocean travel and an ingrained appreciation for the animals that live in the sea, developed communications with the sea animals, including the whales and dolphins, but also with other species, to assist them in navigating the waters, leading them to food sources for the voyages and to take back to their cities and a host of other practical purposes. This is really the Telepathic Network at work here: the network of communication used by consciousness in the creation of realities.

If you can now refer to our discussions of consciousness evolution as more resembling a holographic continuum than a linear progression, you may perhaps see what I am driving at here.

The animal and the human are connected. In this case, the human and dolphin and whale are all on this same continuum throughout time, throughout space as you know it. You could say that a "fragment" of the human consciousness of the Atlantean explorers exists within the collective consciousness of the dolphin and the whale. This was true then. This is true now. This is true in your perceived future. Your modern day admirers of the dolphins and whales as "teachers" within non-physical reality are remembering these linkages from their perceived past. Currently these essential relationships exist for you and may be used as gateways to greater understanding of your world and the world of the animal.

Physical Characteristics of the People

The people of this civilization were of varied body types, of course, yet for the most part you would notice the Nordic features in these humans: fair skin, blonde and red hair, slender builds. Many had strong jawbones and quite prominent noses. Blue eyes predominated yet there were also green and even hazel eyes here. This human form might be described as the prototype for the Nordic peoples who would come later, we are speaking now of some 20 thousand years and more before your Christ drama.

The Atlanteans existed then as fervent explorers of both the physical and non-physical worlds. They were, as a race now, quite intelligent in so far as the intellect is concerned. They also cultivated a sort of "natural" intelligence, an intuitive understanding of the way realities are created. This knowing sense was obvious in the countenance of the Atlantean citizen. The adults projected an intensity of personal power, you might say, to those around them. There was at that time, within the Atlantean culture, a mutual respect for the individual. There was not the prevalence of racial prejudice, hatred, anger, that sort of thing. These emotional complexes were to gain ascendance much later, in other civilizations on Earth.

A Typical Day

In my autobiography we cover the Atlantean existence of ours. Here we shall speak briefly on a typical day within this Mystery Civilization. A moment…

Atlantis as a collective was in many ways further advanced than your present modern societies in the USA, Europe and elsewhere. Mark is struggling here with this description. Let me simplify... Within the spacious moment, i.e., the eternal moment of the enlightened human, ALL civilizations exist. Simultaneous Time is your baseline for experiencing all of your lives.

So for example Mark, you are typing into your computer my messages, now, in your current existence as my collaborator. You are also, within this moment, utilizing communication technologies quite similar to your Internet and other computer services, within the life you lived and indeed I Seth lived, within the Atlantean civilization. I repeat, there is a similarity of Reality Construction within ALL of your existences. You are typing into your computer NOW. In our Atlantean life, you are using a device we have mentioned before, that is powered by crystal technologies, to record your literal thought energies into a physical form for storage. The Atlanteans perfected a method for tuning-in to the subtle energies of thought, and recording this information stream. Typing into a computer was not necessary there, you see. The transcription of thought into manuscript was instantaneous with the use of these devices.

Now not only do your activities in physical reality reveal similarities on all levels, but you may find correspondences at all levels of consciousness manifestation. In this Atlantean life, you Mark are also a scribe for the non-physical beings. This is, in a sense, a "career path" for you over your many incarnations.

The correspondences are apparent to the nth degree. Anywhere you would care to look within your other life, you would notice the correspondences to your current life you are living within your current timeframe.

Now to continue, you are using your crystal device in Atlantis, even as you attend to other activities and obligations there. You Mark currently are contemplating what to have for your breakfast. You are hungry and you are visualizing possible combinations of foods to prepare, while you type into your computer. In this other life, you are engaged in a similar visualization. However in this Simultaneous Life in Atlantis, the process is simplified also. The preparation of the desired foods in the preferred way is accomplished automatically, you might say.

Manifestation Process

The Atlanteans were well versed in the manifestation process. They realized that they could individually use their creative mental apparatus to manifest desired objects, including breakfast. The average human was quite capable of materializing the breakfast with very little physical effort on their part. The cooperative network of Consciousness Units that comprise breakfast were facilitated into their existence within physical reality by human consciousness. To an observer from your timeframe, this would appear as miraculous, magical and so on. Yet wait a few years and you will witness this phenomenon in your perceived future incarnations on Earth. (humorously)

In your progressed future on Earth, it will be commonplace to materialize your thoughts instantaneously, just as the average Atlantean. Mass consciousness, in this instance, the collective consciousness of the Mystery Civilization of Atlantis, co-exists with the mass consciousness of your present and future timeframes and the mass consciousness manifestations that exist within these timeframes.

There are bleedthroughs on all levels here. These occur in the moment, the spacious moment that connects all realities, all timeframes, you see. This is as much as I can tell you about the recreation of past civilizations in your perceived present and future timeframes. There is more information on this matter to be obtained on the subtle levels using your Inner Senses. I direct you therefore to your meditations for further investigations.

Seth, if there were not the emotional complexes of hatred and anger in the consciousness of the Atlanteans, does this mean that the claims of some researchers that "Black Magicians" from Atlantis were instrumental in the down-

fall of the civilization and these beings currently exert an influence upon our world cultures are not true? MF

Black Magicians of Atlantis

These effects of negativity are the results of the activities of the Negative Entities. These Entities exist out of time, they reside off of the space time continuum Mark. In this way these influences are felt within any peoples, from whatever past, present, or future timeframe you are describing, when the human individuals recreate within their mental environments the negative states. Your media have named these Entities the Black Magicians of Atlantis, apparently, however, these Entities have also gone by the name Annunaki, as in our previous descriptions, and by, as I said, the multitude of names relating to the negative gods and goddesses, spirits, ghosts and what have you. It is all the same energy, however, Mark. The imagination of the individual marks this perceived energy with the particular attributes and characteristics of familial, tribal, country, world personalizations of these energy gestalts.

The Black Magicians of Atlantis, then, were inspired, enlivened, empowered by the same energy that drives the personifications of the devil gods, the goddesses of destruction, and so on, within your religions. It is all the same energy. It is all a part of All That Is – the great consciousness Entity exhibiting itself within physical reality through the activities of human and other beings.

Now with regards to the comments on anger, hatred, and the like. A moment…

I refer you to our discussion of the best case scenario, the ideal of the individual, the society as a whole, the world culture, that exists within the pre-manifestation domains as a potential for those involved. You Mark and your colleagues in physical reality exist within your collectives, of whatever type and stripe. You and your mate create your ongoing relationship according to GOCs within your consciousness representing all of the "good" AND the "bad" that life has to offer.

Here, the good may be described as Loving appreciation for your mate, shall we say, and the bad may be described as thoughts and feelings of anger, denial, fear, and so on. These GOCs assist the human in the creation of realities on all levels within all collectives. Your relationship, Dear Reader, if it is of a wholesome Loving nature, reflects your reliance on these "good" aspects of consciousness. Now if your relationship was one of hatred, constant negativity in thought and emotion and behavior, you might be said to be focusing on the negative GOCs in your reality creations with regards to relationships. In the BIG relationships of society, country, global collectives, then, you also have your collective reliance on different GOCs

– negative, positive or somewhere in between, and of course these influences fluctuate throughout time.

A Choice

Do you see how, even though in your current relationship, in your current family, in your current world culture, <u>you may be</u> experiencing the predominance of the negative, that the OPPOSITES OF THE NEGATIVE most surely exist for you and your people with just as much potential for manifestation?

The Atlanteans, to get back to the question, were diverted *en masse* from their collective manifestations of peace, Loving Understanding, abundance for all, and so on, by the influences of the Negative Entities, your so-called Black Magicians. In a similar way, in your current timeframe, you as a collective of humans – world humans – are being diverted from your potential trajectories of positive development <u>to the negative</u> by these same Negative Entities.

CHAPTER FOUR

GA

Seth, you said in your second book that you would have more to say about GA in your future manuscripts. Would you say more about GA now? ~ Mark Frost

I shall, certainly, however let us first present for our readers a summary of what has gone before in our descriptions of the divine matriarchy. A moment please…

This collective was first a matriarchal expression within human society. What you would in modern times call the "feminine" aspects of consciousness predominated in all social structures. Women took on the dominant leadership roles, for example, within families on the small level, as well as within the political organizations on the larger level, you might say. We have stated before that there was no competition in GA, as you might conceive of this concept currently. There was no "battle of sexes," as you moderns refer to it. Cooperation was key, here, and ALL personal aspirations were sublimated towards the success of relationships within all spheres.

The men were predominately builders and practitioners of the various trades. Women took on leadership roles in all relationships, modeled after the mothering role of mother-to-child. For this reason ,the society in a business and personal sense was suffused with tenderness and an all pervasive sense of Loving Understanding.

Now the females modeled this unconditional Loving Understanding for the others. In a sense, you could say that when others saw the power, the grace, the extreme utility of this Love in action, they felt entirely justified in sublimating their own desires for the common good, the greatest good of all.

These are primarily dark-complected humans we are describing. If you may think of the current Romanian peoples, you may get a feel for the physical appearance of the GA peoples: Black curly hair, for the most part. Dark colored eyes. Stocky builds generally for men and women. Defined musculature. Indo-European characteristics.

Their Origins

From star systems, predominately Arcturus, and the life-sustaining bodies within that complex. This should not surprise you. We have many times affirmed that ALL of you are from outer space. (humorously)

A Normal Day

Now the normal day would depend on the occupation of the inhabitant. Let us choose a female of moderate rank in the educational establishment. As we said, healthy, Loving relationships were the ideal to strive for in all realms of activity. In the average day, then, this human would – taking her responsibilities quite seriously – prepare for the following day's lessons with these goals in mind: whatever increases Loving Understanding among the students will be accentuated. Misunderstandings of any kind will be "healed" through interventions of various types, including telepathic assistance from teacher to student while in altered states. The uncommon trance, as we have described elsewhere in my new books, was practiced by everyone in the society. Group cohesion was affirmed in this way.

Lessons – academic and social/ethical – were transmitted to students ongoing. During the dreamstate the teacher would present to the student's dreaming consciousness, what you might call "coming attractions" describing future lessons. Then, when the student attended the class in physical reality, they would again enter the uncommon trance and continue the Lesson. In this way knowledge was gained quite naturally in the waking, sleeping, and Trance states.

Please note that many of you are still involved in these types of instruction during altered states. However, for purposes of maintaining your focus in Third-Dimensional Reality, you must usually create amnesia around these experiences. As you may notice, the lines between sleeping, reverie, and waking were not as clearly defined for the GA residents, as for you, Dear Reader.

The Language

They spoke Sumari, for the most part. This is the same Sumari I described in my messages to Jane and Robert. It is a language of Love, quite literally, as we have said. There is a "lightness" to it, and a sense that you understand the emotional content, as a modern observer now, even though you do not understand a word of what is spoken. The telepathic messages are received regardless of having any knowledge of the language itself.

In my work with Jane, it was thought that an understanding of Sumari was attainable only by Jane; that she was the only person who could speak and translate the words. Yet now it can be told (humorously), that ALL of you have the potential to speak and understand this language in your current existence. It is the language spoken and understood in the non-physical worlds, for example. All of you know this language. Again, you have felt you must create amnesia around this fact, to protect your current reality creation. Please know that times have changed. We shall have an experiment shortly, to give you the reader a chance to "remember" your facility with the Sumari language.

Can we spell out the entire name for the reader? ~ MF

G for Gematri. A for Arssa. GA. Mark, the name is not stable at this time. It evolves as everything evolves. You are changing the past through your input in the present.

Now in the Sumari language the name was Gematrie Arssa – Literally, Loving Land. However, the spelling is mutable. What you have there will suffice for now.

Sumari was the primary spoken language. The written language was diverse and quite different across the continent, the European continent, as you know it today. The intentional telepathic communication we noted, involved images and emotions primarily with the capacity to trigger memories, even neuronal growth in the brain. Healing at a distance, as you now call it, was accomplished through this medium.

I mentioned earlier that GA was FIRST a matriarchy. Indeed, this was the most powerful and extensive matriarchy your world has seen. Your myths reflect the heritage of this ancient civilization, particularly the Greek and Roman mythologies. Though GA predominated on what is presently the European continent, through bleedthroughs the Greek and Roman cultures were "seeded" with the matriarchal concepts: the idea of a strong, female goddess, the concepts of democracy as extolling the highest good for all concerned, and so on.

Subjective History

Now GA did not exist as a pure matriarchy for the extent of its reign upon the European Continent. The country was forced to defend their extensive borders from infiltration by warring tribes of various types and nationalities. This is the way it was, in fact. However, let me take a brief side road here in my explanation. I will ask you to conceive of what you know of human history, what you have read in books, learned in school and observed in your dramatic representations, as a highly subjective and romanticized portrayal of what actually occurred. You may know that the history of the world is the history of the victors. It is the winning tribe, country, civilization that "lives to tell the tale," so to speak. Typically, the historian has a cultural bias. They have created their "truthful" depictions according to their own perceptions within their individual Personal Reality Fields, you see. This is the way it has always been done. And so your written histories are lacking in truth, always.

To put it another way here: your history books and portrayals will NEVER be able to give you a comprehensive view of even one second of historical experiencing by an individual, much less a country or people. This is because, please remember, everything that has a probability of happening, does indeed happen. And so if you were to document the history of even one second of the world, to be comprehensive you would have to document the multitude of probable experiences, thoughts, images and emotions entertained by this single human. This is a fine point, to be sure, yet I trust I have given you some perspective here in our analysis.

Decline of GA

The story of the decline of GA is quite similar to the accounts you read in your history books of the decline of any civilization. Forced to defend its borders from attack by less developed humans, less socialized humans, the governing body was obligated to divert resources to security matters, rather than education and the other perceived "healthier" concerns. It is an old story. Eventually, over several hundred years of matriarchal rule, the advantage was lost on the Northern borders of the territory. Though the GA were fierce fighters when defending their land, once the boundaries were breached by the warring tribes, it became more common for the intruders to be taken into the culture and "forgiven." Inter-marrying occurred quite naturally along the borders of GA. This tendency to absorb cultures from without continued until a homogenization of cultures occurred.

Yes Mark, connect the following to the previous post on untruthful histories.

Now continuing here… Without generalizing too extensively here, the tribes that infiltrated the GA borders were comprised of humans who practiced a patriarchal religion. A wrathful vengeance-seeking god was favored by these warriors. The men were asked to support the patriarchal god of war as they went to war. As is usually the case, this was a system created by priests within the tribes, who sought political power to complement their perceived spiritual power.

The GA forces were quite integrated. Men and women served in the country's defense.

As GA absorbed surrounding tribes, the countries and peoples you know as present-day Europe were created. Much of what you know as Western Civilization is based upon a matriarchy, not the patriarchal concerns that predominate now.

The Shift

The Shift to the positive that is occurring in your dimension is largely a RETURN to the practices of the GA civilization. This is a cyclical manifestation that is being experienced by you as a people. Most of you have lived and are living in GA thousands of years ago NOW. Most of you have consequently experienced lives of Loving Understanding and Courage: the hallmarks of the GA civilization. Most of you are conversant in Sumari, the predominant language in GA. The old ways, what we refer to as the Ancient Wisdom, are the ways of the GA civilization.

Additionally, GA was the source of many of your myths concerning the magicians, the divine kings, and so on. Magic was practiced by the majority of the population and because everyone in the culture appreciated and condoned this practice, the magic "worked." The cosmology or belief system of the average GA citizen, you see, supported magical practices and so the collective realities experienced by the citizens of GA comprised a magical reality: one in which miracles did indeed happen; one in which healings of self and others did indeed occur; one in which Lack and other negative realities were, in a sense, "banished" from the collective experience of the people. Evidence of the GA civilization was destroyed by religious leaders. Practitioners of the patriarchal, vengeful god-centered religions were absorbed into the culture, and grew to influence the religions of GA.

The Religions of GA

In a sense, you could truthfully say that the foundational tenets and energies of Christianity, and indeed of all of your World Religions, originated in the divine matriarchy. This makes sense, does it not? The cradle of civilization, then, including the religions of all of the world, was this matriarchy we are calling GA. It is the mother that gives birth to the child; it is the matriarchy that gives birth to society and the world's civilizations as a whole. Period.

Quite naturally now, and conversely here if you follow my reasoning: within linear time, within the evolution of cultures, within this melting pot of GA, the patriarchy made itself known through the actions of humans who resisted the notion of the ascendancy of the feminine generally, but particularly in the religious and political domains.

Notice here that we are not ascribing competing values to the matriarchal and patriarchal concerns. Both occur within your system of reality. Both are valid expressions. However, if you remember our assertion that the human is born, quite literally, out of Love: the all encompassing Love of All That Is, you may also remember that the negative emotions and all emotions in between Love and hate are also experienced while living the life. In this same way, out of a desire to know itself to the nth degree - to the ultimate perimeters of consciousness, you see - All That Is sought to create "tension" within the creative domain of evolutionary consciousness manifestation, by embodying itself in the form of humans behaving in ways different than Lovingly and Courageously. Thus, a different perspective was formed within individual consciousness, within tribes, within the smallest most elementary forms of society. A choice was created. The choice was between Loving Understanding and Courage or fear, anger and everything else in between the two polarities. In the case of the GA civilization, it was quite abrupt, the transformation. There was a critical mass achieved within the population once a majority of patriarchal god worshippers was reached. Almost overnight, you might say, the change occurred, and it was experienced within the collective consciousness of the GA people that an era had ended. A paradise on Earth was no longer possible. I hope you sense my irony in this last statement.

Borrowed Concepts

Now: it is well known by researchers that the Christian principles, imagery, and so on, were borrowed from preceding spiritual practices, including, of course, the GA religion. Obviously, the founding priests heavily elaborated on the original Christian ethics established by the Energy Body known as Christ. Before, I have reminded you that the fundamental tenet of The Christ was the all-important Love concept. That was it. It was a simple pronouncement; that with Love of self, of your colleagues in the world, a successful life could be experienced.

Now the priests ignored the original statements of The Christ and other founding energies, of the importance of the "multiple lives" concept. They rejected this foundational principle in favor of an "everlasting life" that the devotee was to experience upon their transition after having lived "a life without sin," or at least a life that included atonement for sins committed.

The creative priests did not have to look far for the patriarchal elements to add to their model of Christian practice. The warring tribes that were inculcated into the GA culture brought with them several differing pantheons based on vengeful patriarchal gods. These warring tribes were on missions from their territories to conquer the people and to obtain land. They were on the offensive, then, while GA, for the most part, merely attempted to defend herself against encroachment by the aggressive warrior tribes.

Seth can you elaborate on the GA religion as it existed before this material, so we will know what you are referring to? ~ MF

Old Time Religion

Mark, here is my elaboration on the GA religion. You are quite right, it should come before the material just covered. The spiritual practice, the religion if you prefer, of the GA peoples was primarily what we have called the Old Time Religion in our new messages to humanity. It is the foundational structured religious practice that gave birth to, or you might say, served as the model for, the practices of magicians, shamans, witches and healers that come with all established social orders. You do know that all cultures, all civilizations contain within the ideal manifestation of the Wonderworker, the magical ancestors, and so on.

All cultures throughout time, then, including the peoples developing in territories out side of GA during that epoch, were and ARE influenced by these magic principles, what many call in modern times "the perennial philosophy." We have elaborated on these originating concepts in our book *Thought Reality,* and I refer you to that manuscript for more information on this subject.

Now, though we have commented on the patriarchal energies in what may seem to be a critical fashion, please know, that within the original GA religious practices, the masculine energies of manifestation were given equal placement within the imagery and rituals of the GA religion.

You may see this egalitarian expression of the Divine within the practices of magicians, shamans, witches and healers in your current timeframe. These sacred concepts and images survive the ages intact, via bleedthroughs, because of their truthful potencies. You sense the truth and power in these representations of the Divine with your Inner Senses. They resonate with the beholder. You are transported to the divine realms of understanding simply by observing the imagery and engaging in the ritual practices.

In our book on *All That Is* we presented an exercise in perception in which we asked the observer to look in front of them and attempt to see All That Is. We suggested that ALL of probable reality that exists in the current moment exists there in front of you for you to see. Yet your perceptual blinders - your beliefs, your issues, your Lessons - prevent you from seeing ALL that is. And so you see a very narrow view of reality in front of you.

Fine-Tune Your Perception

Let me use this exercise in a different way here in our discussion of the Mystery Civilizations. Now: you look in front of you wherever you happen to be. Mark, for example, is looking in front of his picnic table on which he writes on his computer on the deck in the woods behind his house. Mark sees a beautiful landscape before him: the Konocti volcano, many fir trees and some walnut trees, the other homes in the area as well as a glimpse of the beautiful lake that lies a mile or so away. This is what Mark sees, and you Dear Reader, naturally are seeing something else in front of you. Now for my point…

What you see in front of you is your view of All That Is, interpreted through your Lessons, your beliefs, your issues. So you are seeing what it is possible for you to see here, according to your beliefs. If you are of a modern mindset or cosmology, I would guess that your perceptions do not include non-physical beings emerging from the trees, or gigantic crystal transmitters sparkling in the distance. Briefly, what we are saying is this: your perception of your current existence is a focus ON your current existence, yet it could just as easily become a focus on your existence within, for example, the Mystery Civilization of Atlantis, in which we assert there does indeed exist gigantic, black crystal transmitters and receivers. Or let us say you change your focus a bit and pick up on your existence in an aboriginal culture in which you did indeed perceive the Spirits of trees and other objects. You could see the personalization of the spirit energies and you communicated with them.

Now let me be blunt. We have suggested to you that space and time are mere conveniences for you in Third-Dimensional Reality. They are useful for those of you creating lives within the linear time conceptualization. Yet ALL of your existences are "out there in front of you," right where you are now. In other words, you need not travel to France to tune-in to a life you lived in Paris in the 17th Century. Because of the telepathic holographic nature of the CUs that comprise your reality, everything exists at once, and so all of your lives, including those lived in the Mystery Civilizations, exist at once, all in the same "place" at the same "time."

This is a difficult concept to embody, perhaps, and so I shall go further here. Your world, your personal Reality Field, is an illusion, Dear Reader. You create it out of "whole cloth," to coin a phrase, through the energies of your Soul Self. Yet the life you are living does seem solid and convincing, does it not? Your life seems to be more than a group of ideas. It is convincing, it is authentic, it is a realistic (humorously) portrayal of your Issues in dramatic form in physical reality.

It is convincing enough to keep you focused in the current existence and not spinning off into some Simultaneous Life you are living elsewhere in another time. Yet the boundaries of space and time are loosening with these practices we are teaching you. Slowly, I am sure, most of you are learning how to keep a foot in both worlds. Now for some experimentation...

Not each and every single one of you, the readers of this new material, have experienced lives in the GA society. However, most of you have done just that. Before we have an experiment that we first offered in our book on **Soul Evolution** in a general attempt to contact the Mystery Civilizations, consider this: do you tend to be a lover or a hater; a mystic or a cynic; a student or a soldier; a helper or a taker? Are you intuitive or do you fancy your-self an "empirical" scientific observer of the events before you? Do you see where I am taking this? If you do, let us now have our experiment, with the specific purpose of tuning-in on probable lives lived in the Mystery Civiliza-tion we are calling GA.

Experiment - Tuning-In on the GA Civilization

Hypothesis: using your intent in the moment-point allows you to tune-in on other timeframes

Here we are using the term "tuning-in" in a spe-cific way. This relates to our suggestion in the last few books, that the researcher in experimentation with the non-physical reality, use the essential metaphors. Tuning-in refers to the Radio Dial metaphor that we offer as a simple, powerful visualized device that will allow you to ritually bring in the frequencies of the non-physical beings, for example, in a sense, tuning-in on their waveband. This technique works quite well also with the Simultaneous Lives. It is simply a per-sonalized metaphor that you may use to give some context to these metaphysical pursuits. Of course, you may use your own techniques, if that serves the purpose here. Let us begin.

Then simply relax. We are assuming you have, as my student, created a Ritual of Sanctuary for yourself, so that you may safely and without anxiety or fear of any kind, explore non-physical reality.

Perform Your Ritual of Sanctuary

If you have yet to create this Ritual, please envision a golden, protective field around your physical body construct. Nothing harmful may enter this field. You are therefore protected, and you may even take this protective state with you in your outings in waking reality.

So relax and move your body in such a way as to elicit relaxation. You are in your state of Sanctuary. You may now surrender to the healing forces of your greater consciousness, your Soul Self. As you let go in this way, the good feelings build within you. You can feel the ecstasy below the surface that supports you in your Earthly existence. This quest is a very natural one for you. You have been doing these types of experiments for many lifetimes. You are the type of person that enjoys finding out about your unknown lives. And so you can easily use your Intent here to direct you.

Focusing on your goal, allow yourself to drift slowly and easily toward a recognition of the life you are living in GA. This is a matriarchy. The feminine principle, as you understand it, is accentuated within your personal consciousness. Tune-in to that sense of affirmation for the feminine, perhaps visualizing a radio dial before you, and seeing the dial turn to the marking GA. As you turn the dial, images may come to mind. You may hear voices and feel a variety of emotions. Keep our intent on traveling toward the good feeling generated in GA on your radio dial. The good feelings may now grow noticeably. This may signify that you have reached your goal. With your Intent, stop your voyage and rest within the good feelings.

If you have reached your destination: look down at your feet. What type of shoes are you wearing? Look around you. What do you see? Find a mirror or something else that will reflect your image and look at your reflection. Are you male or female? What age are you? And what is your name? Do you remember the Sumari language?

You will have complete recall of all that you are experiencing. When you come up to surface awareness, you will easily be able to remember what you have experienced here.

You may certainly use this experiment when exploring any of the Mystery Civilizations we have noted in this book. The techniques are the same. Simply focus with your Intent on the name of the MC and the feelings emanating from that MC. Each MC has a distinctive vibratory signature that you may tune-in to with your human consciousness. These energy signatures create their own distinctive emotional states. You will, of necessity, have to experiment with these states and follow your own Inner Guidance in these matters.

When you have finished your investigations for this experiment, gradually return to surface awareness. Document your Findings.

Findings _____

_____

_____

_____

_____

CHAPTER FIVE

The Hunza

Are the Hunzas in the mountains of the Himalaya considered a mystery civilization? ~ Kathleen Watson

Teachings of the Masters

The Hunza are technically NOT a Mystery Civilization, for much is known of this collective within the "historical record." However please allow me to comment on this people as representatives of what might be called the "original" teachings of the Masters. The Masters are those Teachers who come into your reality every few thousand years on Earth.

Now it is well known to you that a personality known as Christ presented himself to the people of the Middle East some two thousand years ago. Also it is well known that, around that same time, other Teachers, other Masters incarnated into the societies of the Asian continent and others. Muhammad was another Teacher incarnated about the same time. The Buddha and the Buddhist teachers are quite well known as having influenced the peoples in Asia. These are all known to you, no doubt, as a spiritual practitioner and as a student of religions generally.

However, please note that during this incredibly fertile period that witnessed the propagation of these various paths within the world community, OTHER Masters, OTHER Teachers, also came into physical reality to inform the members of thousands of other collectives upon your planet. We are speaking here of small tribal units on your African continent, as well as large congregates of spiritual practitioners within your aboriginal tribes in Australia, for example.

The Christ

Of course the reason you are not as familiar with these other Masters, is that you are a product of your Western Civilization. You take as fact what you have learned in your Western schools. You have perhaps been brought up within a mainstream religion, such as Catholicism, and have not thought of what other just-as-powerful and valid demonstrations of the Divine there have been elsewhere, in other countries. You have tunnel vision here. I will attempt to rectify that somewhat in the next few pages.

For your information, at about the same time two thousand years ago, Masters and Teachers related to what we are calling The Christ in these books, entered into the bodies of humans within your dimension. Their stories are the stories of the magic ancestors that we have documented in this book. Their stories are the legends of your gods and goddesses as well as Gods and Goddesses with a capital G. All of these beings began their lives around the same time, for they were observing great cycles of incarnation and development.

Again, without lapsing into the metaphysical and etheric too much here, let me just say that these beings were/are Light Bodies, essentially. They did and do now exist as the repository, in a sense, of the spiritual, arcane practices and potentials of humans throughout your perceived past.

The Unknown System

For the most part, these beings lived within other star systems, other dimensions of reality, before coming to the Earth plane to develop and grow. These other systems are the Arcturian, the Sirius system, and the presently unknown undiscovered system that will be identified by your astronomers in your lifetime, Mark.

Now can you imagine these separate, distinguishable repositories of spiritual essence - the Gestalts of Consciousness we are calling Light Bodies - as representing, not only the humans existing within the Asian continent, for example, but extremely well-defined "to the nth degree," such that an emissary from the Divine was created from the collective human thought energy of members of individual small tribal units, as we have stated, and then, in a sense "summoned" to these individual territories around the globe?

If you are poetically inclined, you might say that a "call" was put out by humans everywhere around the world at that time two thousand years ago, to the specifically appropriate Light Body that held within it, again, the hopes, dreams, spiritual essence, of those particular people, to come to their aid.

Earth in Upheaval

During this time, the Earth was in upheaval in a social, religious, and political sense. The old ways were failing in all institutions, including remember, the basic structures within small tribal units. The cycle of development of humans upon the Earth was at a point in which more "information" was necessary from the Logos, you might say. A new energy, a new system of thought was required to take the place of the crumbling systems of order.

Because evolutionary consciousness - All That Is - does not seek its own annihilation, but rather a continuous development to all points of probability within all dimensions, these divine emissaries were sent into physical incarnation to "save" the planet, to save humanity. These rescue efforts of All that Is survive within your spiritual traditions in the documented mythological adventures of the rescuing gods and goddesses of the pantheons of the Greeks and Romans, for example, but also you see, within virtually ANY world religion from ANY of the thousands of collectives of humans throughout time.

As an aside, you are currently at just such a crossroad in your development, when you as a race are calling out to the Divine to be "saved;" saved from your own negative manifestations. (humorously)

Tibetan Buddhism

May we now return to the Hunza to complete this essay? Certainly at about this same time - two thousand years ago in the Himalayas - the residents gave out a call to All That Is requesting a different system of thought, a different essence, you see, that would assist them in guiding their people down a more progressive avenue of creation.

Another aside here... In my books with Jane, I spoke of the Tibetan Buddhism concepts as being the nearest description to the way reality is created by consciousness. The emissaries of The Christ incarnating within these collectives of the mountain peoples were successful, in that the concepts of Reality Creation were taken in as truth and embodied by the human practitioners "whole," so to speak, without embellishments by priests and others. Because the people practiced in isolation, for the most part, from their colleagues in other parts of Asia, they were able to keep the teaching intact. You could say that the Tibetan Buddhist concepts are closer to the truth of the matter, therefore, than the practices of the mainland Buddhists. It was true then and it is as true now.

Certainly the student may explore the Tibetan Buddhist path and see for themselves the obvious correlations between my theory over several decades and the concepts and practices espoused by this group, and kept without alteration over the centuries. That is as much as I will say on this matter for now.

CHAPTER SIX

Lemuria

Would you like to discuss Lemuria today Seth? You said that you would say more eventually. ~ Mark Frost

Proving Ground

Yes Mark. A moment please... We covered Lemuria briefly in our books on ***Thought Reality*** and ***Soul Evolution***. We maintain that this Mystery Civilization is one that exists as a "proving ground," so to speak, for the mythological concepts and personalities of your world's cultures. It does exist in the same sense that ALL supposed, theorized, or visualized societies exist, in so far as they are given consistent thought energy by humans and other forms. This disclaimer applies to all of the theorized collectives we discuss in this volume. The civilizations exist first in the imagination, and are then "fleshed out" with the manifesting energies of people everywhere.

We also referred to Lemuria as the "place" where the seekers of visions and meetings with the non-physical beings go in their ritual journeys. The shamans, visionaries, and other seekers throughout your perceived past, journey to theses uncharted territories of consciousness. Each journey to this underground of the imagination by human visionaries, adds to the storyline and the character development, you might say, of the Lemurian legend.

The Underworld of World Civilization

And now a sideroad: If you were to think of the World Civilization as you are experiencing it now, what would come to mind for you? Many thoughts and images come to mind, I am sure. Now to get a feeling for Lemuria, simply consider the underside, the unspoken reality of your progressed modern culture. In other words, for every remarkable technological advance, let us say, in your modern world, there is a corresponding remarkable advance in this underworld with regards to the natural, non-synthesized, expressions of technological improvement. You would have, for example, the proliferation of advanced forms of communication in this exterior world of the modern Earth, and on the interior, in the land of Lemuria, you might see the counterpart to this technological advance in the form of superior expressions of telepathy, natural communications, you see, that do not require the sophisticated instruments developed by the modern human. This is a science of mind as compared to a science of machine, here.

Another way we have described this is that what we see in the Third Dimension as the Underworld or non-physical reality, is in Lemuria, the ongoing physical reality: the only thing there is, you see. The outer world of 3D Reality is expressed inwardly in the non-physical world of Lemuria in every way, shape, and instance.

These are difficult concepts to express, however, I believe it would help if you would let go of the idea that the non-physical worlds or dimensions look <u>exactly</u> like the myths and other stories of the imagination expressed in your movies and other media. You might even have an advantage if you were to dispense completely with the name Lemuria, for this name is not the one accepted currently.

Ancient Wisdom in Mythological Form

Now in so far as the development over time of the Lemurian expression is concerned, we must go back to the formative years of your world civilizations. As, for example, the European civilization developed from distinct, small tribal collectives into larger groups of humans, what we are calling the Ancient Wisdom was kept alive and transferred to succeeding generations through myths, legends, song, and other social media. Each separate tribe, then, had their own particular expression within the mythological world, for the precepts of the Ancient Wisdom.

It must be said, that in these days of long ago, the mythological realm and the activities of the gods and goddesses, Spirits, and what have you, were quite well-known to the average citizen. The spiritual world was just a gesture away for most people, and all members of the group were steeped in the traditions, rituals, and other paraphernalia of their respective religious traditions.

Now compare this with your modern experience. The Divine is quite far removed from your everyday life. Indeed, the spiritual is divorced from your mundane existence. You are only allowed to practice your spiritual traditions on Sundays, for the most part, while setting aside the majority of your waking hours for work. It is often only during the dreamstate in sleep that you are allowed your explorations of the spiritual realms.

Fortunately for us in this exploration, it is to the altered state of the dream that we will turn to explore this non-physical Mystery Civilization. For this exercise, you would best be prepared by having mastered the Trance State, as we have presented it to you in our books. For what you are doing in the deep Trance State, is in fact, bringing to you the sleeping-dreaming state of consciousness. This is the "foot in both worlds" phenomenon we speak of in the books.

There is a peculiarity in the manifestation of this underworld for the individual. Often what you may find in your investigations is the appearance of the spiritual heritage of your lives. For example: if you are living a life within a mainstream religion currently, you may be presented with the symbols and other material of that religion's history. If you are experiencing one of your other lives within another religion's context, elements of that spiritual material may come to you through bleedthroughs.

The truth of manifestation in the physical world is apparent in the spiritual practices and imagery of the religious practices. The Ancient Wisdom, in other words, is there for you to observe and gain benefit from, if you can look beyond the additions and elaborations put upon it. Having said that, let us present our experiment:

Experiment - Lemuria is the underworld of the world civilizations
Hypothesis: the repository of the mythological and religious practices of humanity may be accessed in the trance state

Perform Your Ritual of Sanctuary

You are emulating your tribal ancestors here in this experiment. The seeker of visions travels to the underworld through contact rituals enacted time-and-time-again. With your Intent, you simply direct your consciousness to travel in what you might call the non-physical vehicle, down into the Earth. You may visualize openings in the Earth that lead you to your desired destination. Using your Intent, simply means that you keep a simple focus on your destination within your consciousness.

Now you are of good, positive, divine Intent here. We have called this perspective the Divine Will in our books. It is a state of consciousness that is developed over time. Your intentions are good, in that, you are exploring the underworld of world consciousness, with a reverence for the beings that inhabit that dimension. You will find your own way with practice.

When you sense that you have gained sufficient information from this experiment, direct your Intent to take you up to surface awareness. Please document your Findings.

Findings _____

_____

_____

_____

_____

CHAPTER SEVEN

Mayan Civilization

Seth, what would you like to talk about today? It's been a long time since we worked on books.

Yes Mark, if you would like, we could answer the question on the Mayan civilization, your 2012, and so on. Would that be adequate?

That would be great Seth.

Bleedthroughs

Very well. Now give me a moment here to collect my thoughts on this matter... Here with the Mayan Civilization, you again have a society that has been studied fairly thoroughly by your scientists. More is certainly revealed as your archaeologists discover new sites where religious observances were held, and so on. Yet from my perspective, again, as we so often remind the reader, YOU would be better off to use your own Inner Senses to explore this civilization.

Therefore, I would ask you, Dear Reader, to consider our concept of bleedthroughs in this analysis. A bleedthrough is a momentary piercing of the dimensional-veil, that allows the human in your timeframe to briefly observe the goings-on in another time period, most usually for you, from within Past Timeframes. Remember however, that the future is just as easily accessible through the use of your innate perceptive lenses, these Inner Senses.

Point of Power

The bleedthroughs may be anticipated through a form of meditation or Trance. Simply, the researcher "takes hold" of their current Moment Point, creating a Point of Power as I have described it elsewhere. In this moment, the Inner Senses are activated to draw-in data of a visual, auditory, tactile nature, you see, to the Personal Reality Field. This anticipation, as we call it, sets the stage for a bleedthrough event to occur.

Incidentally, this is the exact mental state of the archaeological researcher who makes tremendous discoveries intuitively. They are so engrossed in their studies that they are quite naturally activating the bleedthrough "mechanism" and do indeed obtain the valuable insights into the culture being studied.

Past Life Existence

Now let us assume for a moment that <u>it is</u> your fervent desire to connect with this ancient civilization. Perhaps it is a long-standing dream for you to make contact in some way. You have read stories in your history books and in your media about the civilization and the material resonates with you; perhaps it even evokes momentary bleedthroughs that allow you to witness the activities within that civilization. If this is the case, we might also assume that you have lived one or several of your Simultaneous Existences within this period of history in this civilization.

You have an interest in the Mayan civilization, then, because it is personal: you have experienced lives in that era and you wish to remember what you learned in that era. Perhaps you are responding to a call from that past life existence, therefore, to go back and re-live some of your experiences. This is a common occurrence both forward and backward in perceived time. In this case, you could say that you are keeping an appointment, made perhaps in this lifetime of long ago, to meet up, and perhaps, in a sense, compare notes as to Lessons learned, or avoided, and so on.

Additionally, this civilization has effectively " seeded" your world culture with the elements necessary to experience the required sensory effects to get the message across to you, in a manner of speaking. This is The Shift that has been foreseen by your visionaries. Many books of material have been written on this civilization and the 2012 phenomenon. Your media have proclaimed the importance of 2012 to the world. The stage is set, therefore, within the world consciousness, for this reincarnational drama of humanity to unfold.

This Shift has been foretold in other practices, such as the Hopi way, and so on, such that the time is now right. The mass consciousness is tuned at this time for this particular presentation of the Ancient Wisdom to be remembered and endorsed by millions of awakening humans.

Now you may receive information on this culture and The Shift for yourself in the Trance state. This is a way to avoid the fear and sensationalism that follows these concepts in your modern media.

Experiment - Exploring the Mayan Civilization and The Shift of 2012

Hypothesis: you may experience in the trance state what the shift holds for you personally

Perform Your Ritual of Sanctuary

It is best to let go of any preconceived notions of the Mayan civilization and what The Shift may mean for you. Material that may have come from harrowing accounts of catastrophes that are "destined" to occur, should be intentionally blocked from your consciousness. One way to do this is to allow the negative images to float to the "top" of your consciousness where they can be sifted out, or in some other way, visualized away from your ritual proceedings.

As you may know, we maintain in our new books that The Shift will bring a realization to the individual human of ALL of their Simultaneous Existences. Consciousness is becoming known to itself with The Shift. As that occurs, the individual explorer will begin to experience their other lives with a growing frequency. This exercise, therefore, may be one in which you may explore your personal stake in The Shift. You will be using your Intent here, to direct your consciousness to that divine perspective in which you may see, hear, touch, and so on, the activities within your other existences.

There is a high probability that at least one of your lives was lived within this Mayan civilization. However, be prepared to experience bleedthroughs into multiple existences that you are living in, while you, at the same time, live within your current existence, in this current timeframe.

The process for returning to normal wakefulness is the same as in all of your experimentations. Direct your consciousness to gently let go of your sensory experiencing within the Trance State. Direct your consciousness to come fully up to surface awareness. Document your Findings.

Findings _____

_____

_____

_____

_____

CHAPTER EIGHT

Mu

What about Mu, Seth? Where was it? What was it like?
~ Elise Mattu

Idealized Society

Mu is one of those lost civilizations that you as a race have created from several different civilizations. This Mystery Civilization existed as a prototypical culture within the collective of humanity's imagination.

Now, every collective of humans, of animals, of insects and even of inanimate materials as you call them, every amalgam of CUs has a collective "vision" of itself. Of course, every conceivable vision of Mu exists within probable realities. For our purposes here in this explanation, let us think of the vision as just two fold: There is the "real time" vision, the idea on which is built the CURRENT "bedrock reality" that is experienced by the inhabitants, in this case, the humans of Mu. But it could as easily be the reality as experienced by the atoms that compose a rock upon your lawn. Anything and everything has consciousness and everything exists at once.

Now secondly, each collective, each Gestalt of Consciousness if you prefer, has a vision of the future – an idealized dream or vision of where they would like to be in a future manifestation of their present culture. This future vision or vision of the future is fed by the best case scenarios entertained within the mental environments of all participants in the collective.

Your Mu civilization was just such an idealized society created on the mental plane of existence by the members of a civilization that existed in certainly <u>a far less idealized</u> manner, if I may say so.

I'm getting the name Ahmna? Is that the name of the civilization, Seth?~ MF

Strict Caste System

Let me continue Mark. The citizens of this extensive network of city-states were avid dreamers and visionaries. This psychic aspect of consciousness was stressed over the practical application of physical energy and planning of real life amenities in the AHMNA culture. As you know, realities are created in just this way. Reality Constructs are "considered" into manifestation, beginning in the dream state, and then fleshed out in detail in the waking state. It was of course the same with the people of Ahmna with a critical difference. These humans were so entirely adverse to the feeling of emotions such as pain, frustration, anger and the like, that they almost completely neglected the creation of the vision – the idealized culture – within physical reality and sought to, as a group now, simply focus on this Astral template of an idealized culture. This idealized culture exists as a holographic entity in time within your collective awareness.

Again, the real life physical reality of the Ahmna civilization was quite mundane and unremarkable. There was a strict caste system. There was no slavery, as you know it, but "human capital," to coin one of your humorous terms, was certainly employed by the ruling class. They were quite mystics, most of them – philosopher kings, you see.

Now the idealized vision of this almost feudal system, you can easily imagine. The members of the lower castes would dream of an egalitarian political and social system, perhaps something of a true democracy. So this was entered into the mix. The philosopher king rulers, in their moments of positive reverie, contributed to the vision with dreams of themselves as benevolent masters, loved and cherished by their subjects.

As for physical descriptions of these people, I may tell you that they were similar in facial features to the Eskimo.

The faces were quite darker, however, with flat cheeks small noses, large almond-shaped eyes. The hair was thick and black for the most part. Both men and women enjoyed adorning the hair with clay ornaments, jeweled barrettes and leather ties of various colors. They were a strikingly beautiful people. You may see the vestiges in, as I said, the Eskimo and the far northern Native American tribes.

CHAPTER NINE

The Niamennon and the Origins of the Semitic Tribes

Would you speak on the Niamennon and the origins of the Semitic tribes? ~ Anonymous

Arcturus

This question we shall answer as a way to also address the question of why did the religions grow from particular regions on your Earth. Now the Niamennon are simply one identified tribe of your early settlers of the Middle Eastern parts of the planet. As is the case with all of you, however, these peoples have their origins on other planets. The Arcturus system and the planets surrounding this body, was the originating point for all of what you would call the Middle Eastern peoples.

Remember now my comments that linear time does not exist in the Soul's perception? Consider then a Soul, an Entity, a Gestalt of Consciousness existing within this

71

Arcturian system, that KNOWS it will have a direct hand in seeding the Earth with the sparks of Soul, the essence of itself, for a "future," in your terms, Reincarnational Drama enacted within the collective consciousness of an entire civilization. These types of activities are conceived outside of time as you know it. In this way the Entity is allowed to witness the future manifestation upon the Earth, of the growth of a tribal collective from their original contribution.

This Entity knew, therefore, that they were to contribute to the gestation of what would become several religious movements. This is delicate and difficult information that I am attempting to transmit to you. In the inception of Spirit into the babies being born in the initial transmission of energies from the Arcturian system, each human was made aware, within the experiencing of their Soul, of their destiny, you might say, in this regard. As the human grew to adulthood, they knew that they were to be involved, either in the first incarnation or later ones, in the growth of these religious movements.

These Souls chose to incarnate on your Earth at that time SPECIFICALLY to become involved in these movements. If you can think of The Christ figure, as I have represented this Energy Gestalt in my writings, as being a part of an extended family, a Soul Family, if you will, simply think of these sojourners to Earth as members of The

Christ Entity. They were keeping appointments with one another on the physical plane to engage in the work of establishing these movements.

The Telepathic Network

There existed at that time, hundreds of years before the birth of your Christ and the other seminal religious figures, an affinity of consciousness, one human for the other, such that the Telepathic Network that connects all of consciousness was acknowledged and relied upon for the truth in any circumstance. The mental environment of the average human at the time, then, contained this vital connection to the Divine. Long before the growth of Christianity into a movement, the Semitic tribes relied upon this cohesive force of nature – the communication stream of The Christ Entity.

Now the disclaimer: (humorously) We refer to The Christ Entity as having established on your Earth all of the religious movements. This includes those that grew into the world religions, as well as those that remained tribal-centric, being kept within smaller collectives. We refer to this Energy Body as The Christ, however, you could just as easily and correctly identify this influence as The Buddha Entity, or The Great Spirit Entity, and so on.

Portals to the Etheric

The question as to why the world religions grew from the same locations on your Earth can be answered in this way...

In the original inception of energy from the Arcturian system, it was realized that the Middle East and Far East contained the most positive influences for the establishment of particular religious systems. The manifestation process was and is accelerated in these regions. The portals to the etheric, as I have referred to them in the past, were and are quite open there. Thought is transformed into physical reality constructs quite easily there through these portals of energy exchange: what we have called Coordinate Points. This has to do with peculiarities of the electromagnetic influences that "charge" the environment in this area of your planet. This becomes obvious, if you think about it. For a more comprehensive explanation of this process I refer you to my earlier books written with Jane and her husband.

Now as you know, both the Divine and the not-so-divine are manifested in your reality. Thus, we have the tendency for the negative aspects of consciousness, the formative energies of the negative gods, to be made manifest there as well. This area is a proving ground for the creation of realities from consciousness. As such, both the perceived negative and positive are made known in the physical dimension.

CHAPTER TEN

The Seti

And what about the Seti? Are the Seti remnants of a civilization of "giants" that lived in very ancient pre-history?
~ Kathleen Watson

Probable Evolutionary Paths

In my manuscripts of long ago, I have made note of just this type of experimentation in the creation of the human form. Certainly there have been whole societies of gigantic, in your terms, human beings who were exploring probable evolutionary paths at literally "the same time" that what you would call primitive man was developing on your African and other continents. I remind you that ALL expressions of humanity, of the human form within physical reality, do indeed occur. All possibilities are explored. True, many of these experiments take place on probable trajectories of development, and so are not acknowledged in your consensus reality. Yet through bleedthroughs between these other dimensions, probable dimensions you see, representing other timeframes past, present, and future, developing man and woman did experience glimpses of the divine ancestors, as we have used the term here, and other inhabitants of the adjacent dimensions.

These Seti, then, exist in an adjacent dimension to your Third Dimension, where they developed through your so-called Ages – Iron, Bronze etc. These giants were, of course, thought of as gods by those fortunate enough to observe them within the visionary experience and other altered states. The stories of Sasquatch and other giant humanoids are actually referencing contacts with these extra-dimensional beings.

The Expression of Intelligence

Again, as I have stated in past manuscripts, these beings, though certainly quite "primitive" in appearance, in that they were covered in long hair, wore no clothing, and expressed themselves in a series of grunts and "animal" noises, were of fairly high intelligence. The eyes, you see, expressed this capacity for knowledge, and the expression of intelligence. You could see this potential in the eyes of these beings.

Now they were tool-makers of high sophistication. Though they were not to reach the great heights achieved by other civilizations, they were quite adept at creating from the natural environment in which they found themselves, comfortable structures in which to live, raise their families, and so on.

In a Generalized Fashion

In your distant historical past, there did indeed exist this race of giant, in your terms, humans. They originated, not within any one specific region of Earth, but, if you can imagine this, in a generalized fashion. Again, it is difficult to explain this process of the simultaneous existence of all forms... You are suspended within the coordinates of a space/time matrix. It is difficult for you to step outside of this matrix – the illusion of linear time – and observe All That Is at it creates everything that can be created, including, you see, gigantic humans. In a sense, you could say that your scientific theories and explanations of human evolution, HOLD YOU BACK, prevent you from witnessing your greater creaturehood.

The accepted trajectory of development for humans is quite limited by your myopic scientists. However, if you were to look at your theoretical researchers that have perfected the use of the Inner Senses in their explorations, you would find evidence of this other reality: one inhabited by giants, indeed, as well as many other representatives of the unknown that you currently refer to as the impossible, or perhaps, merely mythological beings. I hope that you notice that this is my disclaimer for the material that will follow. (humorously)

Now the term "generalized"… all probabilities are explored by consciousness in the moment "to the nth degree." Everything exists spontaneously and eternally NOW. The races of humans, all living things, and even supposed inert substances, create themselves in the moment of eternity that exists now.

Let us anticipate your question: "If these other human forms exist now and forever, why do we not know more of them?" Answer: Perhaps it is because you are a modern human. You do not "believe" in these outlandish tales of giants, fairies, angels, and so on. You create your reality through your beliefs. Therefore, you have not participated in the creation of these beings. You have not assisted in their manifestation into your Personal Reality Field.

Now, before I lose you entirely, please remember that the various eras and epochs of time exist as dimensions. We refer to the era that witnessed the giants, therefore, as an alternate dimension, one that you may explore, if you wish, just as you may explore any dimension from within the Third Dimension. Enter into this moment of exploration, then, as I proceed.

The giants were a race of humans that existed simultaneously with all other races. Where all races and nationalities existed, the giants also existed. Thus your legends of gigantic humans who lived on the edge of the village, or in the mountains of regions around your Earth. All regions, all mythologies document the giants. Thus you have your stories of contact, that are in truth, dimensional-bleedthroughs.

Would you like to continue with the giants, Seth?

Yes Mark. I do realize that the "scientists" among you are now scoffing at these descriptions. Scoff if you must. The deniers merely exhibit their disbelief in these matters through denial and intellectualization: "scientifically impossible," you might say. You may now be asking for proof. Let us then go directly to the exercise, where you may receive the proof you require.

Experiment - Contacting the Giants
Hypothesis: the giants of myth may be contacted through experimentation in the trance state

Perform Your Ritual of Sanctuary
The assumption in these new books of mine is that EVERYTHING that can be entertained in the mental environment can attain varying degrees of reality, either in your system or others. You create

your own Personal Reality Field that comprises a radius formed about your physical body construct to about 50 feet. Everywhere you look you create realities there and you have the most "say" in what occurs in your reality within this 50 foot radius. Everything: every atom, every insect, every rock has a reality field in which it exists, for everything is alive. This you should know by now.

Before you, in front of you, right before your eyes, in your Personal Reality Field, exist <u>all</u> of the dimensions of your physical reality that hold <u>all</u> of the humans, animals, trees, and what have you that have existed for eternity. We are speaking of eternity looking forward as well as backward, here. Past, present, and future manifestations of anything that can be imagined, exist right where you are, Dear Reader.

I have described these dimensions as available to you in "layers" of reality. With this metaphor you might conceive of the dimension in which the giants exist as one that lies somewhat downward in front of you, looking into the earth at a 45 degree angle. Building upon this metaphor, can you get a sense of the perspective of peering into other dimensions, by using your Intent now, and focusing the consciousness, the Inner Senses we are talking about now, to bring into clarity the dimension of the theorized giants?

We know from communications with our readers, that some of you have already made contact with these beings and have developed relationships over the years. So this experiment is possible and quite easy to do. It is one that has been used by explorers throughout the ages to perceive the giants and other so-called mythological beings. You are, therefore, taking on the roll of visionary in this experiment. Your imagination will come into play, in the sense that you will be open to the images of these beings. You will use your Inner Sense of sight to tune-in to the dimension in which the giants exist, and then be open to accepting what you are viewing.

Here it is important to remember that you may have preconceived notions of what a giant looks like. My advice is to try to recognize these images as barriers to understanding. The truth of these beings is not romantic at all. Please attempt to look beyond the cultural stereotypes offered by your motion pictures, books, and other media.

Again, when you feel as though you have gathered enough information in your experiment, simply direct your consciousness out of the Trance State and up to surface awareness. Document your Findings immediately, while the information is fresh in your mind.

Findings _____

_____

_____

_____

_____

CHAPTER ELEVEN

The Sumari Family
of Consciousness

Are the Sumari a Mystery Civilization? ~ Cynthia Hill

Soul Family

Many of my readers have fallen in love with my theory of long ago, of the families of consciousness. I did indeed separate out the various types of consciousness expression within humanity for teaching purposes. It was my wish that through describing your differences to you - as in the varying personality characteristics and attributes - I would point the way to a deeper exploration of the self: the Soul Self of the reader.

I assume that some of the readers of my early works have assessed from which of the families they have sprung, and have taken this designation to heart, identified with it, you see, in perhaps the same way that the lover of astrology identifies with the astrological sign and attributes of their birth date and time. How many though have taken the exploration further, to the discoveries that lie within the psyche, within the unknown reality?

Now this is precisely why I have returned with a simplification of my theories. We have dispensed with the families of consciousness and now propose an overreaching concept of Soul Family to describe the interactions within collectives of humans over time. The focus on the individual becomes a focus on the group: the Soul Family.

New Age Movement

However, specifically for our project here, we <u>shall</u> discuss the Sumari briefly. Because this group is primarily composed of the Vanguard we describe in the new material - the magicians, shamans, witches and healers - I feel that we can once again speak of this group. It is germane to this discussion of the awakening of humanity, of The Shift in consciousness, of the remembering of the Ancient Wisdom, and other subjects we focus on in my new books.

What has been called the New Age movement in literature, in the arts, in the social, political, and spiritual arenas, is being driven by the Sumari family of consciousness. You are always instigators of the beneficial and ENLIGHTENING movements of humankind. And so you are again gathering forces in your modern timeframe to remember the Ancient Wisdom <u>together.</u>

Of course it is not enough to simply remember this material and reinforce it among yourselves in the Sumari collective. In order to be effective you must, as individuals and as a collective of do-gooders, see to it that your systems are transformed for the highest good of all concerned. Simply: it is your duty to use Love with a capital in all of your behaviors to humanize all of the domains of human interaction and development. This is what you do, you see, this is your *modus operandi*, so to speak.

To this end, some of you will carry out your duties overtly, as in the practices of the New Agers. You will act in public under the flag, so to speak, of the Sumari: the Lovers of humanity. Others of you that are indeed the reincarnation of this Sumari family, will act <u>covertly</u>, undercover, without fanfare, without notice, really, yet certainly with the same precise agendas as your colleagues: to co-create a Loving world for yourselves, your families, and for all of humanity.

Bleedthroughs

This movement in your timeframe represents a cyclical renovation of the world culture. It would not be over-simplifying too much here, to state that this movement is spurred by a bleedthrough to the civilizations of your past that is being experienced by many millions of you. Again, the human race is at a very dangerous crossroads currently.

MYSTERY CIVILIZATIONS

All of your structures that have previously held you together are disintegrating. The power elite that control your world's resources are resisting any changes to their entitlement: their self-perceived ownership of your planet. As a collective, the Sumari family of consciousness is attempting to spread their influence throughout the world, allowing these potent ideas of change to energize the greater collective of humanity. It is a time of potential revolution you have before you, nationally and globally. You can sense this potential, can you not? The Ancient Wisdom is being remembered and honored. The rights of the individual are becoming paramount. The collective is becoming empowered as the inefficient social systems of the past regime fall away.

Remember here, this is how civilizations are created. It is always an inside phenomenon. The non-physical world creates the outside physical world, always. The best practices, in a sense, that have created positive value for civilizations in your past, are being remembered. Therefore, go to your dreams and reveries and witness the Mystery Civilizations as they give birth to The New World. Help where you can, Dear Reader.

Experiment - Exploring Sumari consciousness
Hypothesis: you may explore sumari consciousness in the trance state

Currently this is a highly-energized Idea Construct within your collective awareness. These values of the Sumari - Love, Courage, compassion, altruistic public service - resonate with the overall collective of humanity at this time, for the ideals of the Sumari are quite necessary for the healing of your Earth and the peoples that live upon Her. On the subtle levels, all of you are aware of this.

Additionally, by identifying with, by allying with, by embodying the Sumari code, so to speak, you become Sumari. What you focus on within your consciousness strengthens and develops in your reality. What may have begun as a simple interest in New Age practices, for example, representing a fragment of Sumari consciousness within your mental environment, may expand as the Sumari aspect strengthens.

Now the language of Sumari is the language of the post-Transition environment. As an etheric being, after your physical death, you use Sumari to communicate with others who have made the Transition and are considering their options as to what lives to explore next. Sumari is the language of the non-physical world. All of you are well-versed in this language, for you have all experienced many deaths, many Transitions, many opportunities to use this language. With this in mind ...

Perform Your Ritual of Sanctuary

As in our other explorations in this book, use your Intent to tune-in to that aspect of your consciousness you identify as Sumari. There is an assumption here that you are reading this book for a reason. It may be that you are keeping appointments that you have made in other lives. Consider what it would feel like to keep an appointment with an aspect of your greater consciousness, this Sumari. In essence, you are using your Intent to remember something here. When you feel you have experienced noteworthy Findings, come up to surface awareness. Document your experiences.

Findings _____

_____

_____

_____

_____

CHAPTER TWELVE

Best Case Scenario

I have a deep and old feeling of life being about everyone winning and the common good being the norm. Seems I could dream a more coherent reality to match my preferred reality. Any help or insights you can offer?

~ Jay O. Wilder

Your Reverie

Yes my friend, let me answer your question in this way... Now you ARE living all of your lives at once, here. You are now musing on the possibility of a better life for yourself, dreaming as you say. However, with a slight altering of perception you could, if properly motivated, tune-in on your life in a probable reality in which you are experiencing a predominance of the common good, everyone "winning," and so on.

You are an authority on your current existence. You know more about it than any other being. In just this way, you are also an authority on this other existence that is playing out in a probable "field" of experiencing for you. It is available for you and you alone. It is your life being expressed as a best-case-scenario, as we have described it in the past.

Your touchstone, in a sense, for voyaging from your current experiencing of a less-than-perfect reality to this probable reality, is the emotional state you describe as dreaming. You might also describe it as a pleasant longing. These are simple techniques here... dreaming, longing; you are essentially using your self-generated positive emotional state as a homing device to zero-in on the probable reality you desire. Your emotional tone will become quite positive when you do this properly.

When you have indeed reached this best-case-scenario life that you are living in a probable reality - remember, all probable realities are explored by your consciousness, in perpetuity, you might say - imagine yourself luxuriating in the influences that create this positive reality. Soak up these positive feelings.

The positive manifestation ALWAYS exists for you as a probability. When you conduct this exercise, you divert your attention from your current moment of creating less-than-satisfactory Reality Constructs, to the creation of positive, life-affirming, ecstasy-filled Reality Constructs. It only takes a moment to improve your reality in this way.

EPILOGUE

Does this or that civilization, though, exist in fact, you may ask? Does your Western Civilization or your American Empire exist? These are philosophical propositions. For the more you explore your Personal Reality in an attempt to find proofs, the more you find that <u>all</u> is composed of consciousness.

Now consciousness, as you know, and as some of your more conscious scientists also know, is limitless. Being limitless it achieves any form. In this view, do you see that the possibility exists for not only these few theorized cultures we describe in this book to exist, but for ALL permutations into physical form, of any and all probable social, political, and spiritual constructs to exist? All possible civilizations exist. Period. All thoughts or images entertained by humans seek out fulfillment in the form of Reality Constructs, including civilizations.

You may take this as a disclaimer, if you wish. Yet it is, you must admit, an intensely empowering disclaimer. It is empowering for YOU the individual explorer of consciousness.

Now I have answered the specific questions you raised and I am not at liberty to elaborate indefinitely. When you can ask the right questions, perhaps in your probable future, Dear Reader, I will give you more information. However, this is a good start.

RITUAL OF SANCTUARY

The Ritual of Sanctuary was presented to readers in our book on **Soul Evolution** when we first began to emphasize direct exploration of the Unknown Reality. We felt that the reader would require some personalized protection in their experimentation.

The most simple form of the Ritual is to imagine, prior to psychic pursuits, a golden Light surrounding you. Nothing harmful can penetrate this field of Light. It has a healing protective influence. You may certainly use this simplified form while you go about creating your own Ritual.

The object here is to generate positive energies with your creative consciousness. Try listing on a piece of paper your positive beliefs and ideas that denote security, peace, and protection. The next step would be to, perhaps artistically, distill these potent concepts down into an image, statement, or physical object that resonates with the protective energies. Naturally you may include gestures, visualizations, or any other evocative materials. Practice your Ritual until you can create at-will the state of Sanctuary within your own consciousness. Only you will know when you are successful.

Glossary
Definitions for the concepts Seth discusses
in this book.

All That Is - The energy source from which all life
sprung throughout the multitude of Universes, transcending
all dimensions of consciousness and being part of all. Also
referred to as the Logos and Evolutionary Consciousness.

Ancient Wisdom - The knowledge of the magicians,
shamans, witches and healers of the past.

Awakening - As the Ancient Wisdom is remembered by
humanity, an awareness of the greater reality is experienced
by individuals.

Beliefs - Ideas, images, and emotions within your mental
environment that act as filters and norms in the creation of
Personal Realities.

Bleedthroughs - Momentary experiencing of lives being
lived in other tirmeframes and other systems of reality.

Co-creation - You co-create your reality with the limitless creative energies of All That Is.

Consciousness Unit - The theorized building blocks of
realities. Elements of awarized energy that are telepathic
and holographic.

Courage - Courage and Loving Understanding replace
denial and intellectualization in the creation of Positive
Realities.

Denial - The ego/intellect prevents the learning of Lessons by denying the truth of the matter.

Dimensions - Points of reference from one reality to the
other with different vibrational wavelengths of consciousness.

Divine Day - The student attempts to live a complete waking day while maintaining contact with the Energy Personality.

Divine Will - The will is potentiated through ongoing contact and communication with Beings of Light. Also called Intent.

Ego/Intellect - The aspect of the personality that attempts to maintain the status quo reality.

Ecstasy - The positive emotion experienced in contact with the Divine.

Embodiment - Precepts are lived in the creation of improved realities.

Energy Personality - A being capable of transferring their thought energy inter-dimensionally to physical beings and sometimes using the physical abilities of those beings for communication.

Entity - Being not presently manifested on the physical plane. Also known as a Spirit.

Fourth-Dimensional Shift - Consciousness expands as the individual experiences an awareness of all Simultaneous Existences. Also called Unity of Consciousness Awareness.

Gestalts of Consciousness - Assemblages of Consciousness Units into Reality Constructs of all types.

gods - Consciousness personalized and projected outward into reality. A self-created projection of the developing ego.

Holographic Insert - Teaching aid of the non-physical beings. Multisensory construct experienced with the Inner Senses.

Incarnation - To move oneself into another life experience on the physical plane.

Inner Sense - The Soul's perspective. Both the creator and the perceiver of Personal Realities.

Intellectualization - The aspect of the psyche that attempts to figure things out so that the status quo is maintained.

Intention - See Divine Will.

Lessons - Chosen life experiences of the Soul for further spiritual evolution.

Light Body - The etheric body of refined light.

Love - Love with a capital A is the force behind manifestation in the Third Dimension.

Moment Point - The current empowered moment of awakening. Exists as a portal to all points past, present and future and all Simultaneous Lives.

Mystery Civilizations - Foundational civilizations largely unknown to modern science. Some examples are Atlantis, Lemuria and GA.

Negative Emotion - Habitual creation of negative emotions creates enduring negative realities.

Negative Entities - Negative energies that roam the Universes in pursuit of their own power to dominate.

Percept - Perception creates reality in the Third Dimension through the Inner Senses..

Personal Reality Field - The radius within your self-created world within which you have the most control in the creation of Reality Constructs.

Precept - Empowered concepts of manifestation. Example: you create your own reality.

Reality - That which one assumes to be true based on one's thoughts and experiences. Also called Perceived Reality.

Reality Creation - Consciousness creates reality.

Reincarnational Drama - Soul Family drama enacted to teach the participants a Lesson in Value Fulfillment.

Scientist of Consciousness - The researcher studies the phenomena within the Personal Reality Field by testing hypotheses in experimentation. See Precept.

Observer Perspective - Self-created aspect of consciousness that sees beyond the limitations of the ego/intellect. An intermediary position between the ego and the Soul Self.

Seth - An energy personality essence that has appeared within the mental environments of humans throughout the millennia to educate and inspire.

Simultaneous Lives - The multidimensional simultaneous experiences of Souls in incarnation.

Soul - The non-physical counterpart to the physical human body, personality, and mentality. The spiritual aspect of the human.

Soul Evolution - The conscious learning of Lessons without denial or intellectualization.

Soul Family - The group of humans you incarnate with lifetime after lifetime to learn your Lessons together.

Spiritual Hierarchy - Beings of Light who have mastered multidimensional levels of experience throughout the Universes and have moved on to higher service in the evolution of all Souls.

The Christ - The embodiment of The Christ in your World. Also called World Teacher. First described in Seth Speaks.

The Council - Members of the Spiritual Hierarchy. Highly evolved beings that advise Souls on incarnations for their spiritual evolution.

The New World - The Positive Manifestation.

The Vanguard - Advocates for humanity and Mother Earth who incarnate together to lead progressive movements of various kinds.

Third Dimension - The physical plane of Earthly existence.

Trance State - The relaxed, focused state of awareness that allows the Scientist of Consciousness to conduct experiments and collect data.

Value Fulfillment - Consciousness seeks manifestation of itself into all realities via the fulfillment of all values.

Visionary - Reincarnated magicians, shamans, witches and healers in this current timeframe.

I think we're going to have to do a book or two or three or four or many more to get the masses to see the problem ... Seth

MORE BOOKS?

Seth has promised to continue to communicate with us to further the awakening of humanity. This means that there will be an ongoing source of current, inspirational messages available from: **Seth Returns Publishing**

Communications from Seth
on the Awakening of Humanity
9/11: The Unknown Reality of the World
The first original Seth book in two decades.
The Next Chapter in the Evolution of the Soul
The Scientist of Consciousness Workbook.
Thought Reality
Contains The Healing Regimen and Spiritual Prosperity.

The Trilogy
All That Is - Seth Comments on the Creative Source
Mystery Civilizations - Seth Answers Reader's Questions on Legendary Civilizations
Soul Mate/Soul Family - Lifetime After Lifetime We Learn Our Lessons Together

Seth - A Multidimensional Autobiography - in 2010

To order visit **sethreturns.com** or **amazon.com** Or ask your local metaphysical bookstore to carry the new Seth books.